JOHN THOMPSON'S
EASIEST PIANO COURSE

PART THREE

PLAYBACK+
Speed • Pitch • Balance • Loop

To access audio, visit:
www.halleonard.com/mylibrary

Enter Code
3283-8871-5859-9336

Illustrations by Sergio Sandoval

ISBN 978-1-5400-1369-9

EXCLUSIVELY DISTRIBUTED BY

 WILLIS MUSIC

 HAL•LEONARD®

Visit Hal Leonard Online at
www.halleonard.com

World headquarters, contact:
Hal Leonard
7777 West Bluemound Road
Milwaukee, WI 53213
Email: info@halleonard.com

In Europe, contact:
Hal Leonard Europe Limited
42 Wigmore Street
Marylebone, London, W1U 2RY
Email: info@halleonardeurope.com

In Australia, contact:
Hal Leonard Australia Pty. Ltd.
4 Lentara Court
Cheltenham, Victoria, 3192 Australia
Email: info@halleonard.com.au

Teachers and Parents

THE PHRASE

Part Three begins by showing the importance of playing and listening to music phrase by phrase rather than note by note. Teachers should emphasize the importance of playing each phrase with different musical treatment — one of the first steps in interpretation.

TOUCH

Touch is obviously a vital part of interpretation; examples in *staccato*, *legato*, slurs, etc. follow in proper sequence. For thorough development of the various touches, the teacher is referred to the author's edition of the *Hanon Studies.*

SCALES AND CHORDS

Scale formation follows the lessons on Half Steps and Whole Steps, with examples using the scale both as melody and as accompaniment figures. Triads and inversions are shown later, with pieces using chords in "block" and broken form. The seventh chord (with its resolution) is not analyzed harmonically, but simply taught as a chord pattern that should be memorized by the student because of its frequent appearance in music at this level.

SCOPE

In key signatures, the book progresses as far as three flats and three sharps. The remaining key signatures follow in Part Four. The scales and chords used in this book are shown on pages 44 and 45. A glossary of musical terms, with abbreviations and definitions, is on page 46. The last few lessons in the book introduce a new time signature – six-eight.

As with the other books in this course, all the lessons are specially designed with short but frequent practice periods in mind.

John Thompson

Contents

The Phrase

Music, like language, is divided into sentences, but musical sentences are called **phrases**.

"Melody" consists of two phrases. Sometimes the second phrase is played louder than the first — sometimes softer. But never exactly alike. How do you think the second phrase should be played? It is correct either way, but it should be played the way **you** feel it.

Always think of music **phrase by phrase**, not note by note. Then you will play with more musical purpose and understanding.

Hand Position

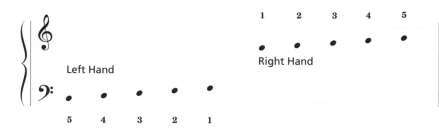

Preparatory Studies

Left Hand   ### Right Hand

Melody

Three Phrases

Here is a piece with three phrases. Try playing it three different ways:

First time   –   1st phrase, very softly; 2nd phrase, louder; 3rd phrase, louder still.

Second time   –   1st phrase, moderately loud; 2nd phrase, softly; 3rd phrase, much louder.

Third time   –   1st phrase, moderately loud; 2nd phrase, softer; 3rd phrase, much softer.

Choose the way **you** like best. That will be **your very own** interpretation.

Hand Position

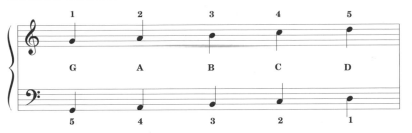

Preparatory Studies

Left Hand   **Right Hand**

The Bee

Folk Song

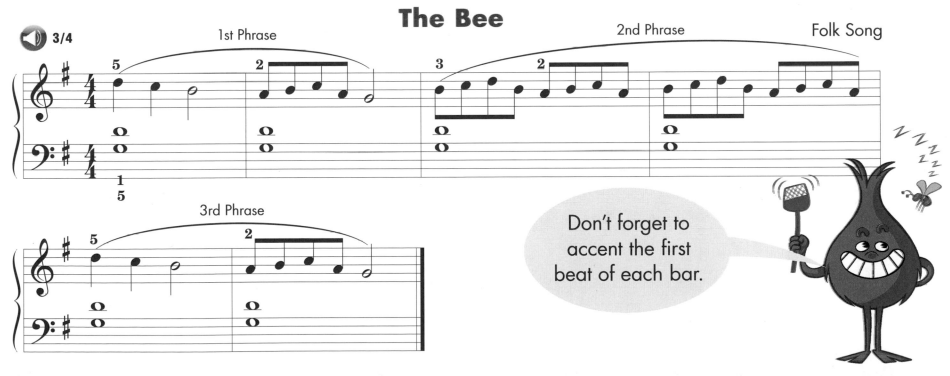

Don't forget to accent the first beat of each bar.

Four Phrases

Always keep a steady, even tempo.

This piece has four phrases. Notice that each phrase is marked differently.

Usually the composer indicates how each phrase should be played.

When no expression marks are shown, play each phrase according to **your** feeling.

The glossary on page 46 has explanations of musical terms used in this book; be sure to look them up.

Much Ado About Nothing

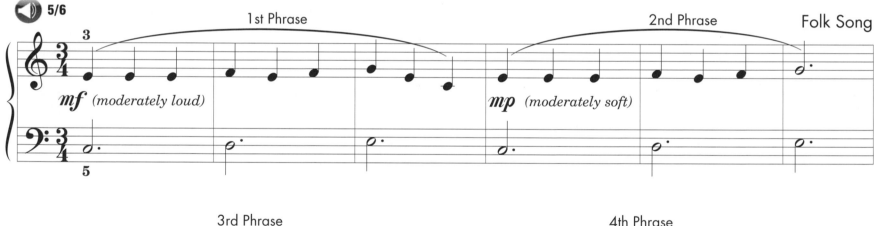

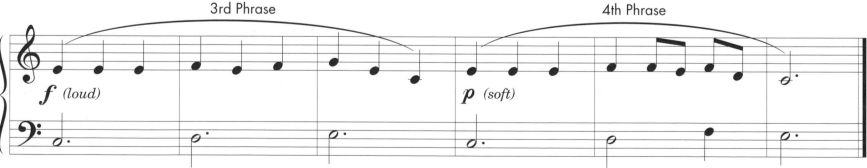

Wrist Staccato

Always be sure to notice the expression marks. See page 46.

Teacher's Note: The subject of **touch** is too important to be covered entirely in this book.

In John Thompson's *Hanon Studies*, specially adapted for pupils at this level, each aspect is carefully explained and developed separately. **Finger, wrist,** and **forearm staccato,** as well as the various forms of **finger legato,** **phrasing,** and **portamento** playing, are all covered in elementary form.

Obviously, touch is a vital part of interpretation and should be introduced early in the student's career.

Demonstrate wrist staccato to your student before introducing these examples.

Exercise in Wrist Staccato

Some Folks Do

Adapted from Stephen Foster

Work Sheet

Naming and transposing the new notes

Write the letter names below:

Writing Exercise

Transpose these notes one octave higher in the bass.

Next, write them in the treble clef. Then recite them as you play.

9/10

At the Animal Fair
Study in Wrist Staccato

Allegretto   Traditional

mp I   went to the   An - i- mal   Fair,   the   birds   and   beasts   were   there.   The

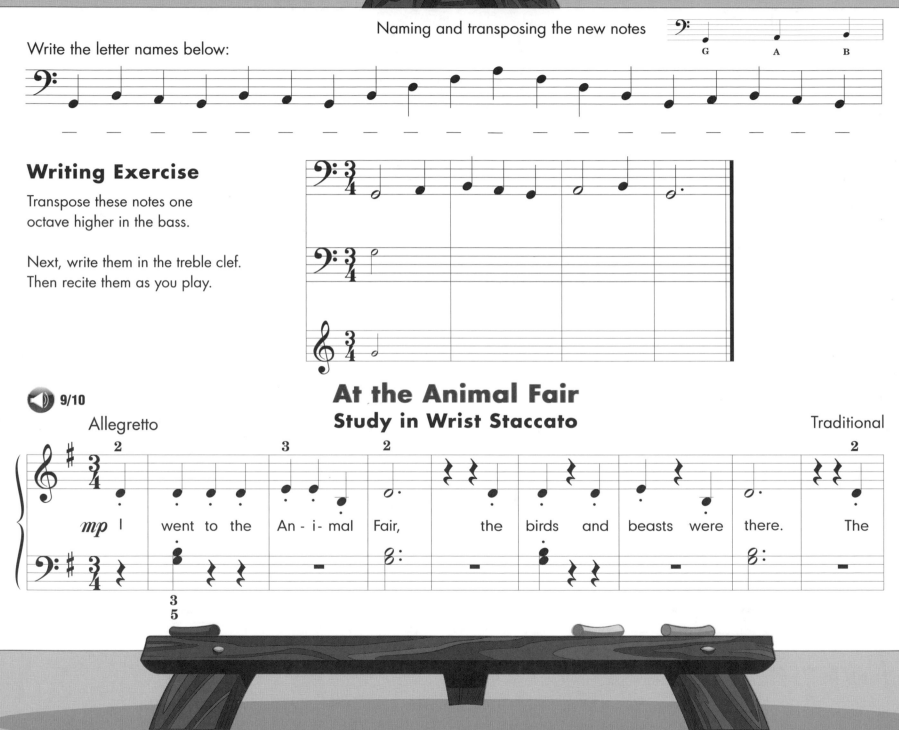

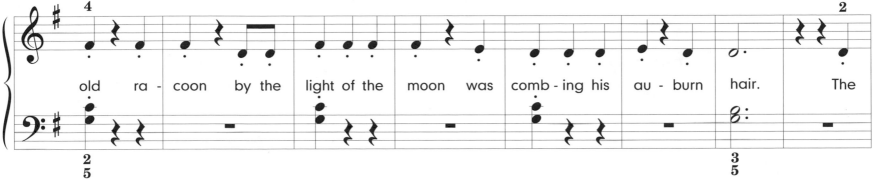

old ra - coon by the light of the moon was comb - ing his au - burn hair. The

mon - key went ker - plunk, fell o - ver the el - e - phant's trunk. The

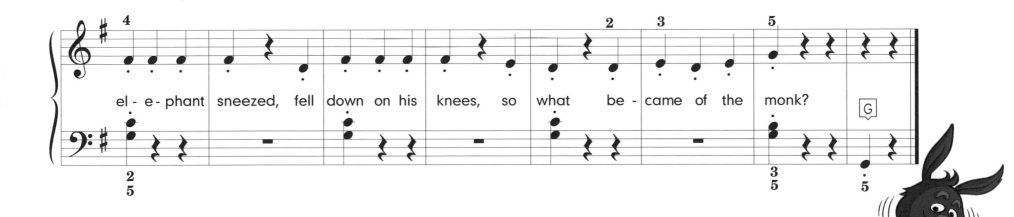

el - e - phant sneezed, fell down on his knees, so what be - came of the monk?

On the Levee

Changing Hand Position

Up to this point, you have changed hand position frequently when moving from one piece to another.

You will find it is just as easy to change position **in the middle** of a piece, and that is what happens here. See how smoothly you can make the change.

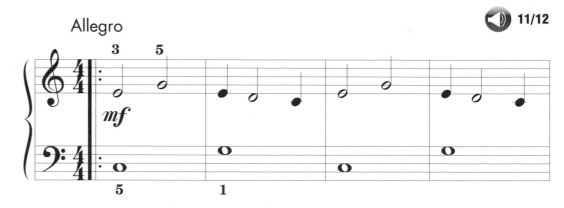

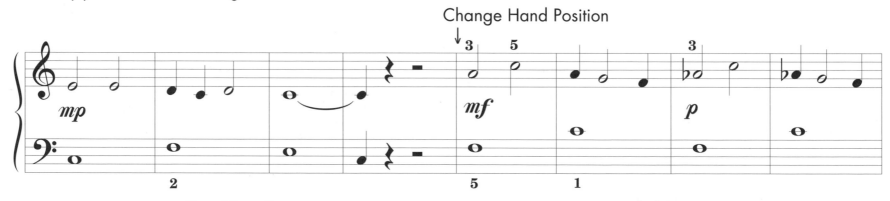

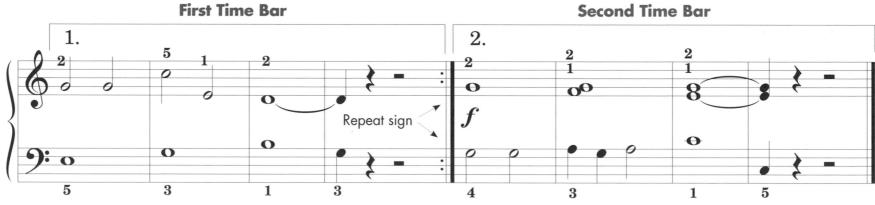

First Time Bar

Second Time Bar

Repeat sign

First and Second Time Bars
From this point, go back to the beginning and play over again. After playing through the **second** time, do **not** repeat the **first time bar**; instead, skip to the **second time bar**.

Sunrise

New Expression Marks

< means a gradual increase in tone.

> means a gradual decrease in tone.

Andantino

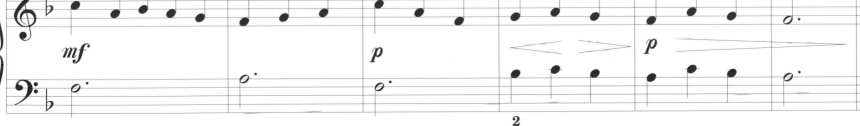

The Slur

Slurring in music is like **breathing** in speech – we take short breaths and long breaths. **Breathe at the end of each slur.** It will strengthen the rhythm and add immensely to the interpretation if you remember to do this.

For **two-note slurs,** think of the words **drop-roll** and the effect will come naturally. Play the **first** note with a gentle **drop** of the arm and the **second** note with a **roll** of the arm and hand in a forward and upward motion, **using no finger action** and **releasing the note** on the upward roll. The **wrist** must be completely relaxed.

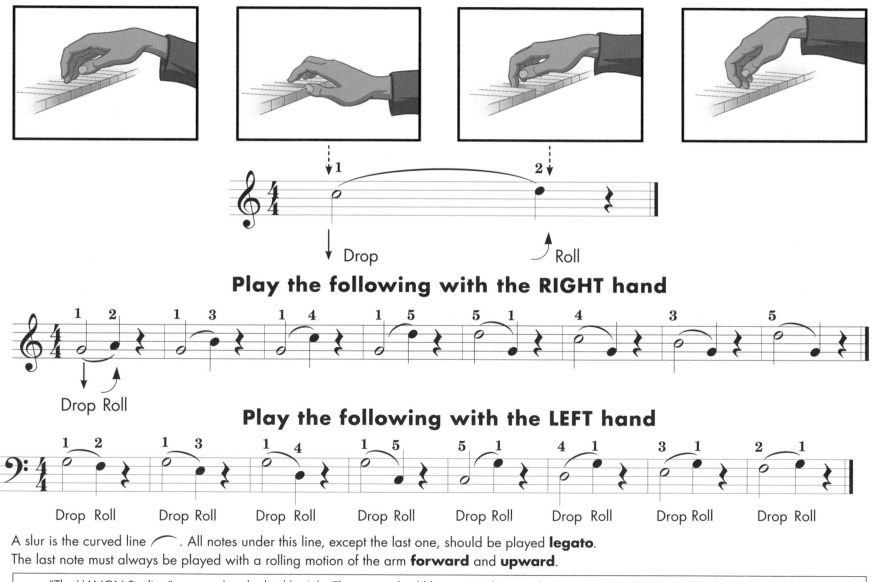

Play the following with the RIGHT hand

Play the following with the LEFT hand

A slur is the curved line ⌒. All notes under this line, except the last one, should be played **legato**.
The last note must always be played with a rolling motion of the arm **forward** and **upward**.

"The HANON Studies," arranged and edited by John Thompson, should be assigned as supplementary work. It is especially adapted to develop the **slurring attack** as well as the fundamental touches used in this book.

Pop Goes the Weasel

🔊 15/16

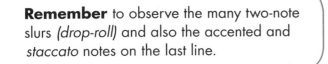

Remember to observe the many two-note slurs *(drop-roll)* and also the accented and *staccato* notes on the last line.

Moderato

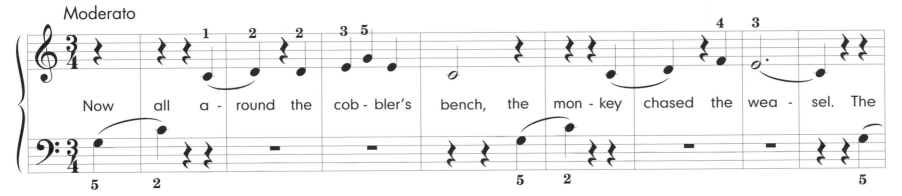

Now all a - round the cob - bler's bench, the mon - key chased the wea - sel. The

mon - key thought 'twas all ___ in fun. *f* Pop! goes the wea - sel.

L.H. over

Accompaniment

Preparatory Study

Right Hand

Left Hand

Boogie Woogie Bill

Allegro moderato

🔊 17/18

mp

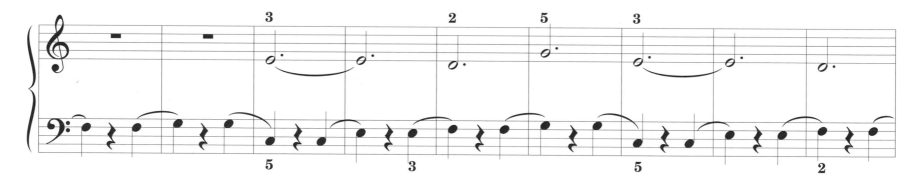

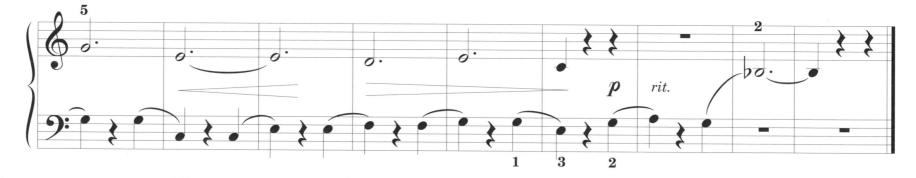

p *rit.*

Robin Redbreast

Allegretto

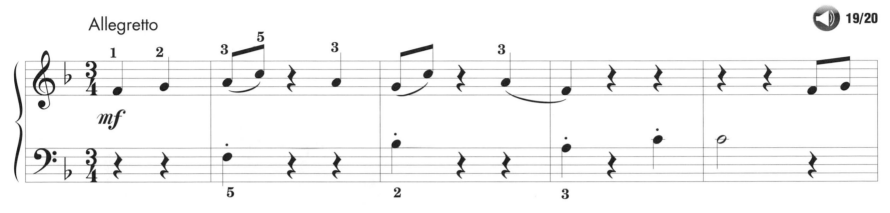

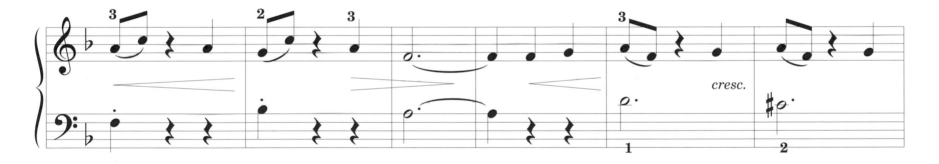

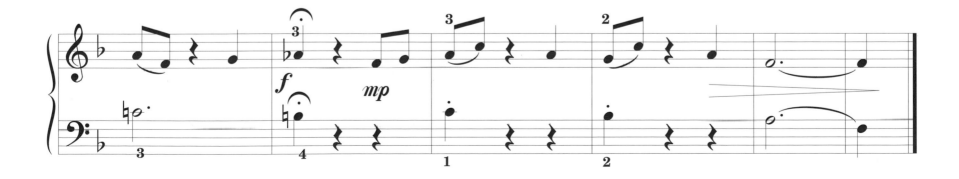

Half Steps

A **half step** is the distance between any key and the next nearest key.
Play the following progression, using the second finger of the right hand:

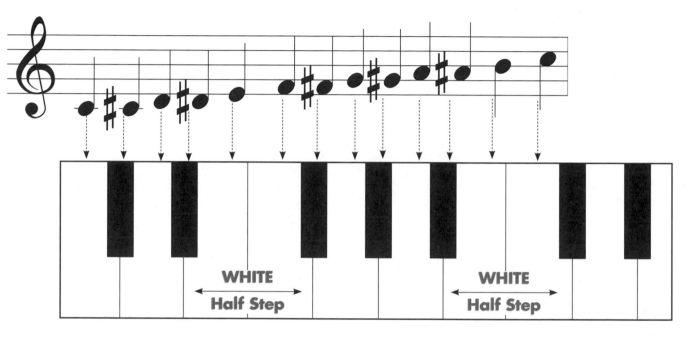

You have just played a series of half steps.

Notice that the piano keyboard is arranged in half steps.

All half steps occur between a white key and a black key, except the white half steps between E and F and B and C.

Play these descending half steps with the left-hand second finger:

Review

You have already learned that:

A **sharp** (♯) before a note **raises** it a half step.

A **flat** (♭) before a note **lowers** it a half step.

A **natural** (♮) before a note **cancels** the sharp or flat sign.

Whole Steps

A **whole step** is twice the distance of a half step: there is always one key – either black or white – in between.

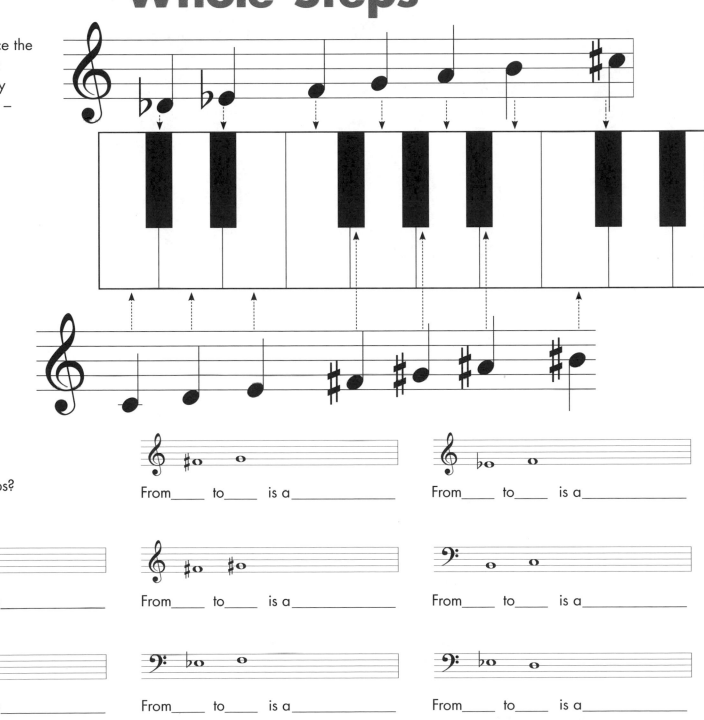

Whole steps and half steps

Whole steps or half steps? Fill in the blanks.

From_____ to_____ is a_____

From_____ to_____ is a_____

From_____ to_____ is a_____

From_____ to_____ is a_____

From_____ to_____ is a_____

From_____ to_____ is a_____

From_____ to_____ is a_____

Three-Note Slurs

Drop, Connect, Roll

Shufflin' Along 🔊 21/22

This is the second "Boogie Woogie" tune. The first was "BOOGIE WOOGIE BILL" in which the repeated pattern was used as accompaniment. Here it appears as melody and is repeated over and over.

To play a three-note slur, **drop** on the first note, **connect** the second with finger *legato*, and **roll** off on the third note.

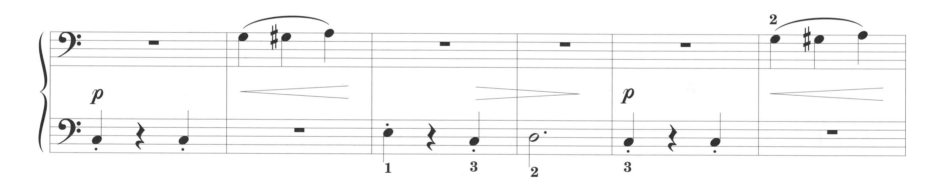

Crossing Hands

Shadow Dance

This piece using crossed hands is built for the most part on three-note slurs.
Make as much distinction as possible between *staccato* and *legato*.
Notice all the expression marks and see if you can imitate the playfulness of dancing shadows.

Animato

23/24

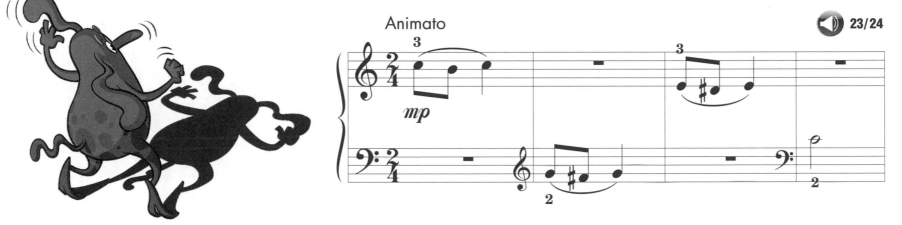

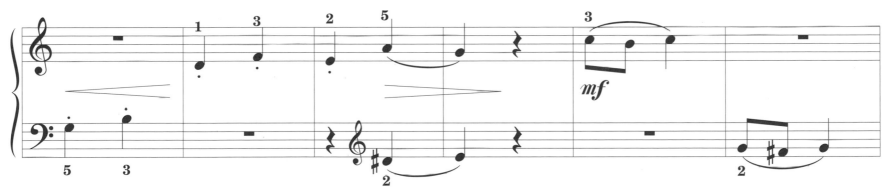

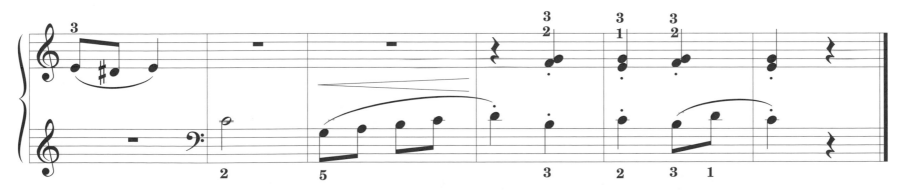

Major Scales

Writing Exercises

A scale is a succession of eight notes progressing in alphabetical order.

The notes are numbered 1, 2, 3, 4, 5, 6, 7, 8 and are known as the **degrees** of the scale.

The major scale contains whole steps and half steps. The half steps occur between 3 and 4 and between 7 and 8, as shown in this example.

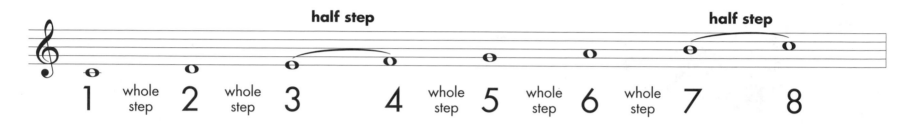

Write the following scales using sharps or flats where necessary to keep the order of whole steps and half steps.

Scale of G Major

Scale of D Major

Scale of A Major

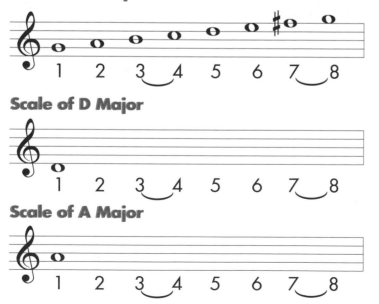

Scale of F Major

Scale of B♭ Major

Scale of E♭ Major

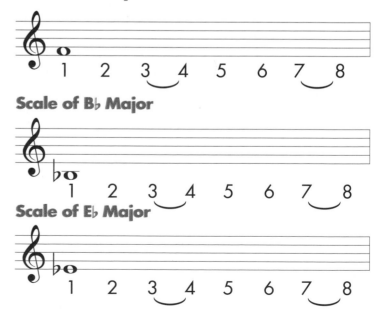

Preparatory Exercise

The Juggler

25/26

New Signature for Four-Four

The sign **c** is another way of showing the time signature of four-four.

In the following example, the G Major scale is divided between the hands and used as melody.

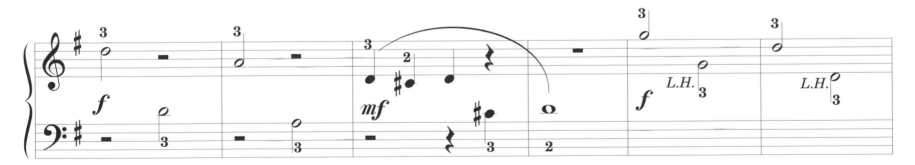

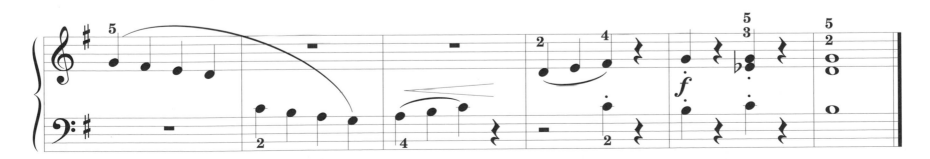

Scale Drill

27/28

Acrobats

Syncopation
I Like Rhythm 🔊 29/30

I like rhythm in all my livin',
A tune with rhythm is just for me.
Syncopation has got the nation,
But it's easy as "A B C."

Syncopation occurs when the normal accent has been disturbed. That is when the accent is placed on a beat that would ordinarily be a weak beat.

In this piece, we find the second beat (normally a weak beat) emphasized by the accent sign. This change of accent gives a "swing" to the rhythm and is known as syncopation.

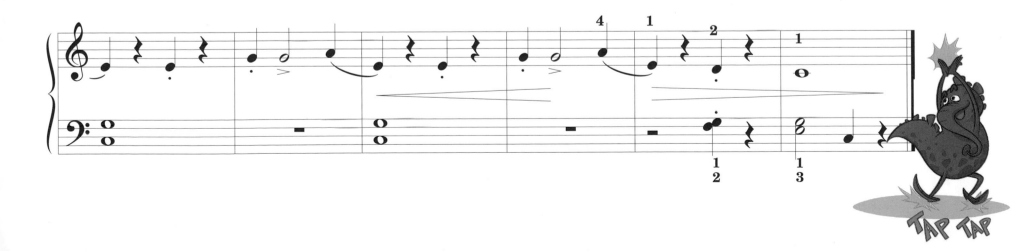

24

Preparatory Exercise

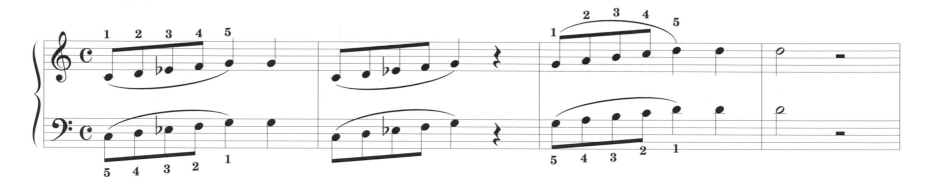

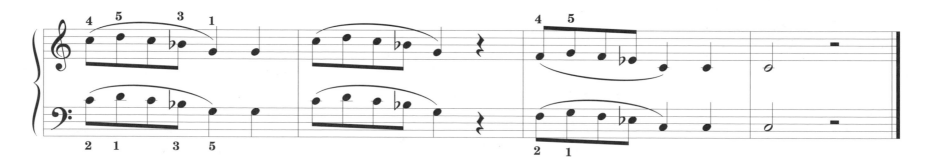

Tribal Dance

Allegro

31/32

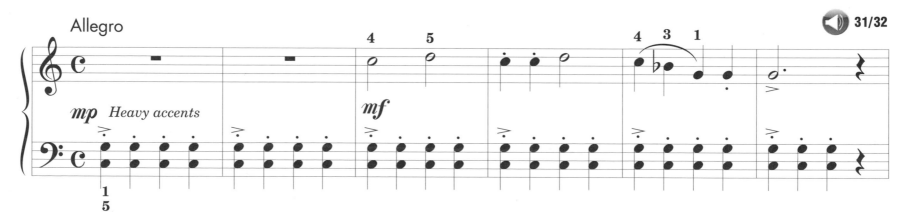

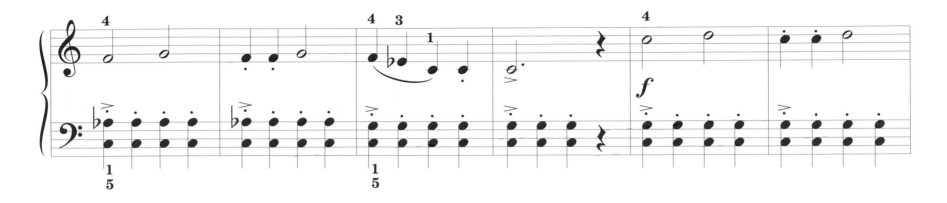

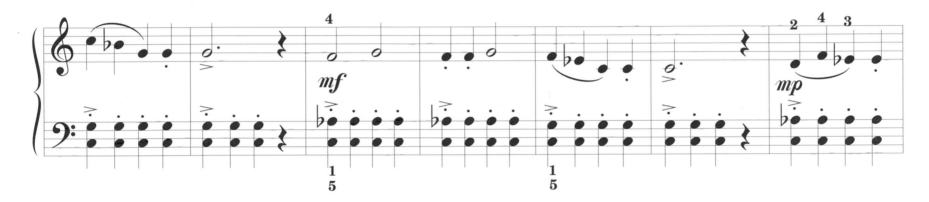

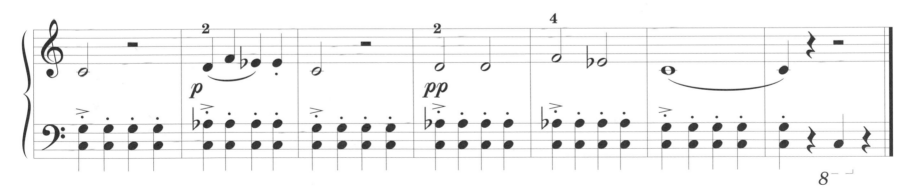

Duet for Teacher and Student
Cake Walk
Secondo

The **Cake Walk** used to be very popular in America. It was performed by couples marching around the dance floor to music. A flag was passed from one couple to the next, and when the band stopped playing – without warning – the couple holding the flag won the prize: a cake! Ragtime music suited the complicated steps and movements that were used by the couples to outdo each other.

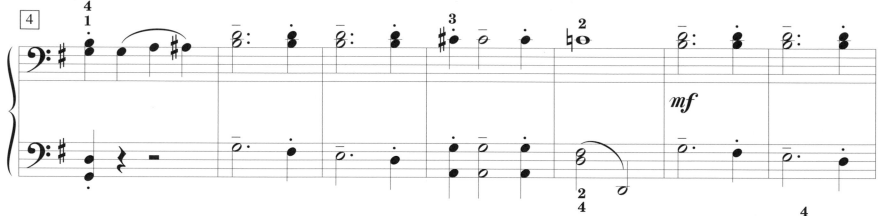

Cake Walk
Primo

33/34

In this example, the syncopation occurs on the last half of the first beat in most measures. Be sure to apply vigorous accents throughout.

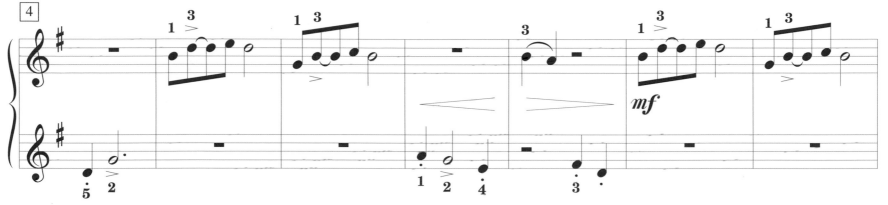

Chord Building

Major Triads

A triad is a chord of **three** notes.

If you take the 1st, 3rd, and 5th notes of the major scale (skipping those in between) –

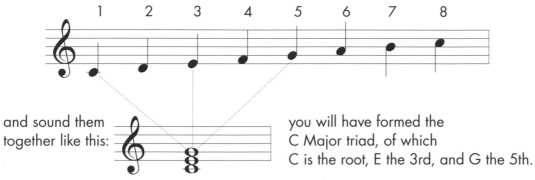

and sound them together like this:

you will have formed the C Major triad, of which C is the root, E the 3rd, and G the 5th.

Play These Triads

The F Major triad

The G Major triad

Broken Triads

When triads appear in broken form, they are known as broken chords or **arpeggios**. Play:

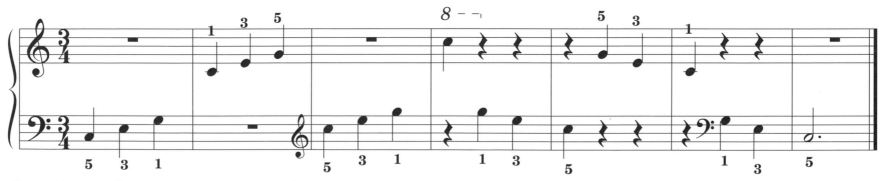

Play F Major and G Major arpeggios in the form shown above.

Inversions

Sometimes the notes of a triad are scrambled like the words in a puzzle – in which case they are said to be **inverted**.

The Three Positions of the C Major Triad

Play with each hand.

Write (and play) the three positions of the F Major and G Major triads –
using the same chord patterns shown in the examples above.

Chord Capers

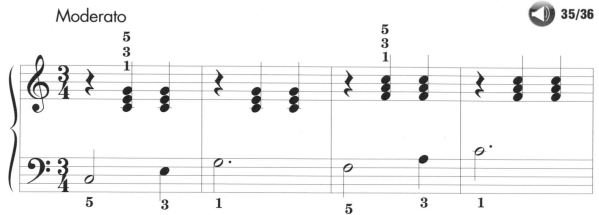

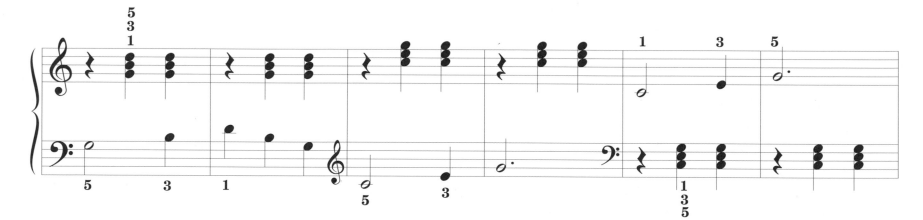

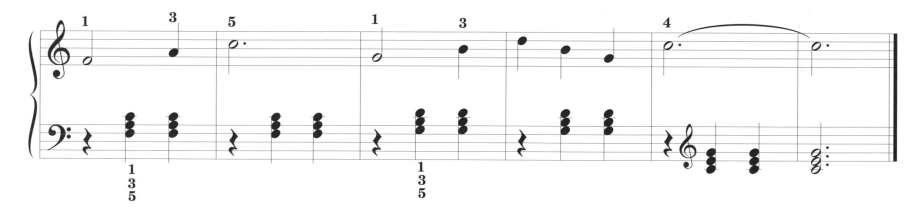

Broken Chord Etude

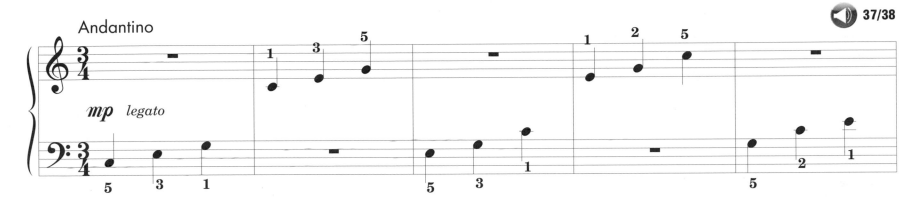

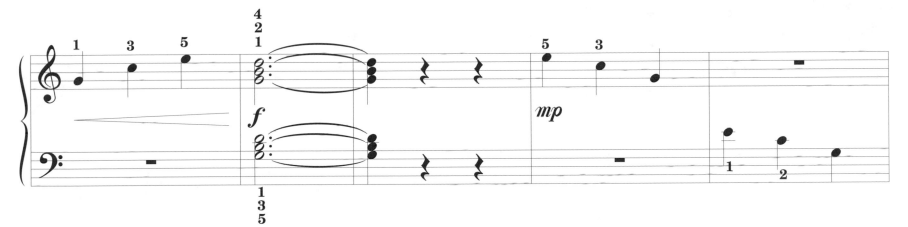

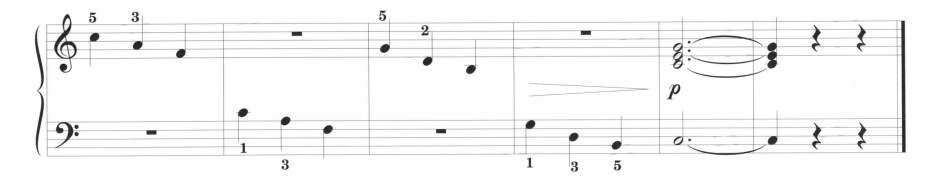

Chord Patterns

Here are some chord patterns that appear often in music.
Repeat them until you can recognize them by sight and
by ear. This will help your sight-reading and memorizing.

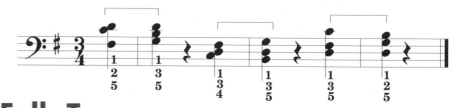

39/40

An Old Folk Tune

Animato

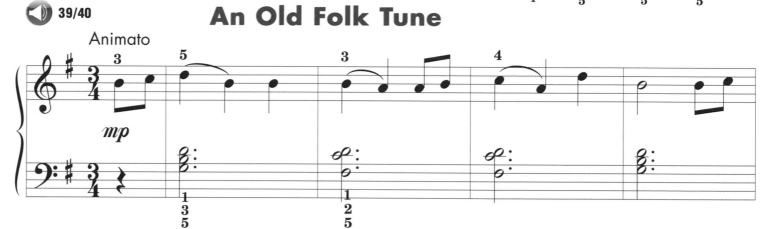

Cross-Hand Etude

Broken Chords

Allegretto

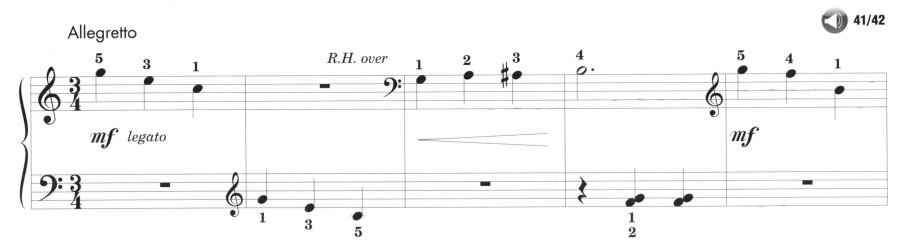

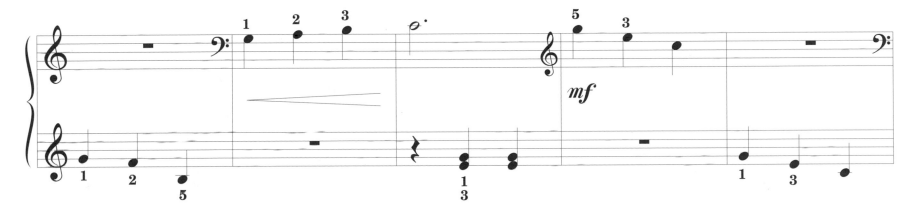

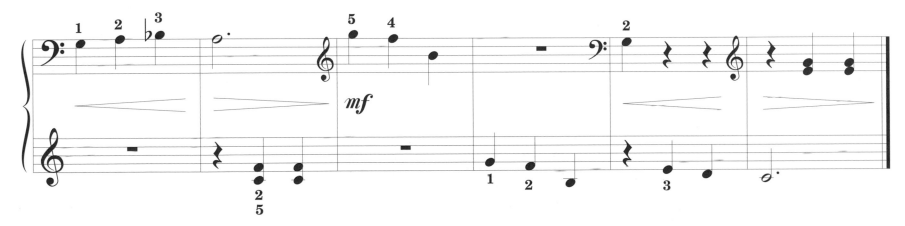

Dissonances
Chinese Theatre 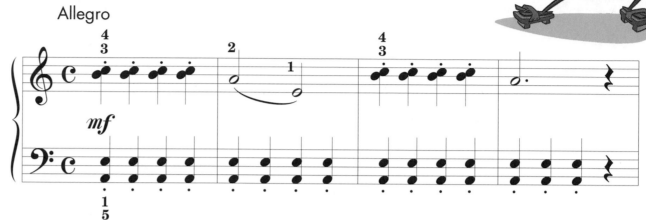 43/44

Allegro

There is a certain beauty
to dissonances that you
will learn to appreciate as
you advance in your
piano studies.

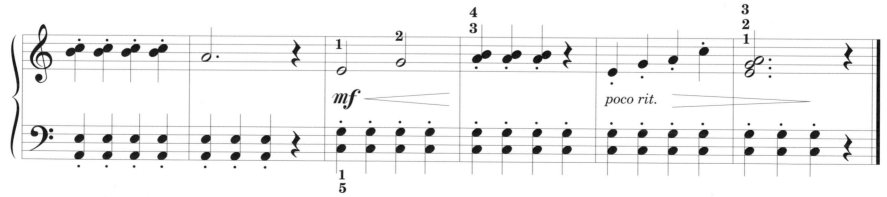

Peasant Dance 🔊 45/46

Play the scale and arpeggio of D Major each day before practicing this piece. (See page 44.)

Be sure to follow the many two-note slurs in this piece. Put sharp accents on the first beat of each measure to ensure good rhythm.

Animato

Folk Tune

Etude in B-Flat 🔊 47/48

Play this etude in two ways. Firstly, as written – two notes with the left hand and three with the right. Then, make a cross-hand study of it by passing the left hand over to play the last note of each measure with the second finger (all measures except the last two). In measures 10, 11, 12, and 13, play the notes with the little lines under them (–) with extra singing quality – like melody notes.

Teacher's Note: Pedal may be used here, once in each measure.

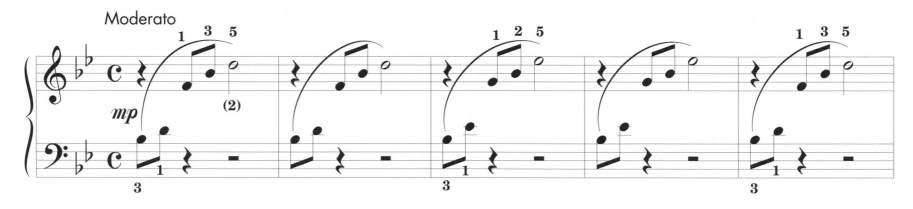

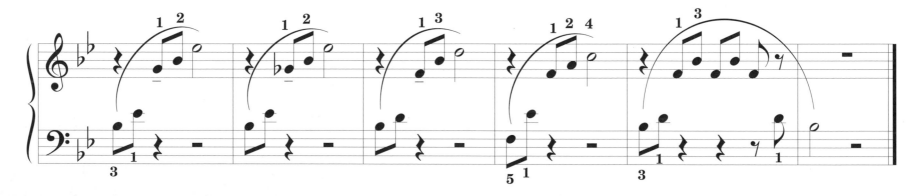

O Sole Mio

Play this old Italian song as expressively as possible.

The left-hand broken chords should be played with a rolling motion of the hand from the fifth finger over to the thumb.

49/50

Allegro Moderato

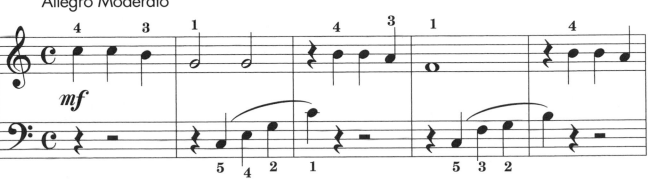

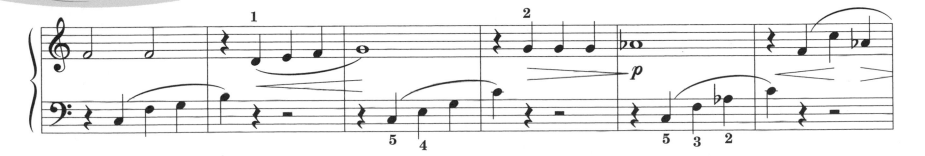

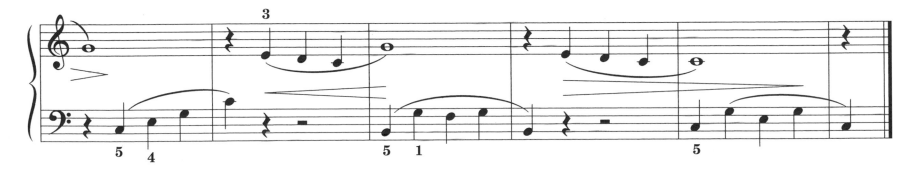

Cowboy's Song

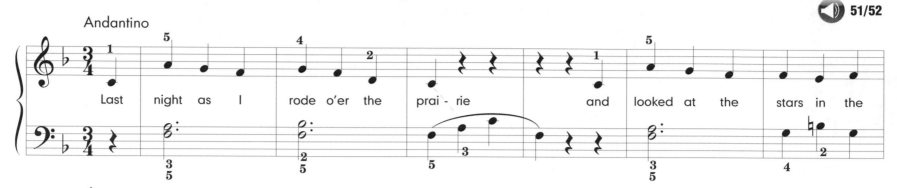

Last night as I rode o'er the prai - rie and looked at the stars in the

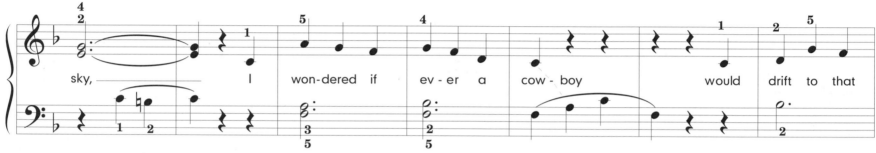

sky, I won-dered if ev - er a cow - boy would drift to that

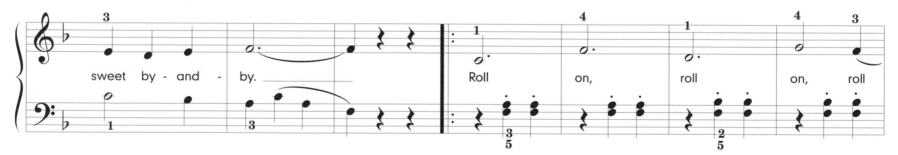

sweet by - and - by. Roll on, roll on, roll

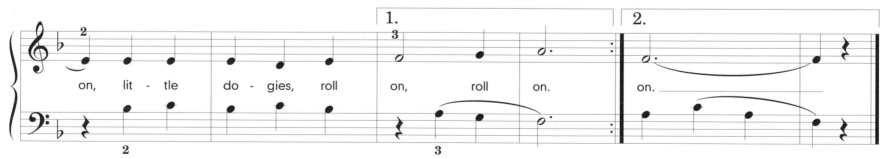

on, lit - tle do - gies, roll on, roll on. on.

A Little Bit of Rag

Allegro animato

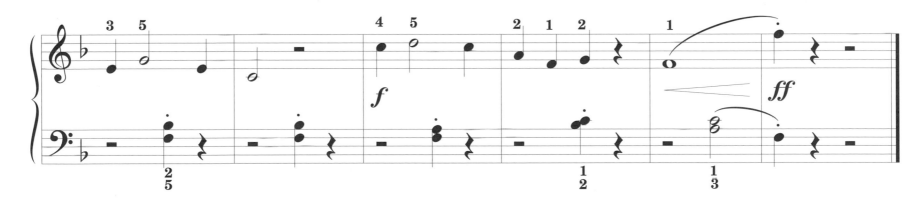

Preparatory Exercise

Holiday Song

Play the A Major scale and arpeggio every day.

55/56

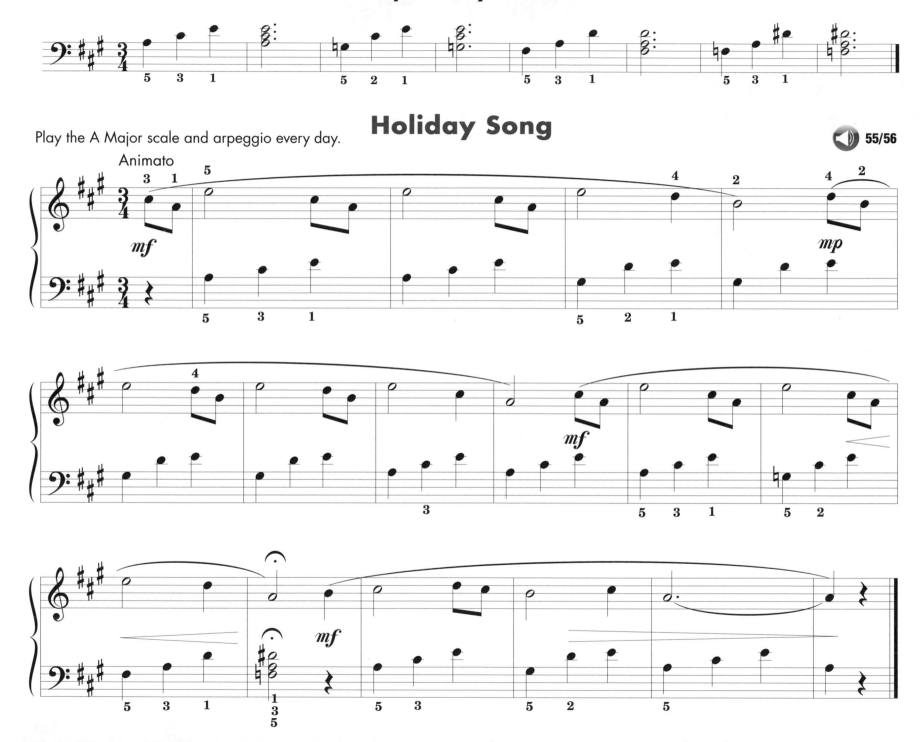

Six-Eight

Here is a new Time Signature which means there are
six counts to each measure and one count to each eighth note.

Tramp, Tramp, Tramp 🔊 57/58

George F. Root

The time values are as follows:

♪ = 1 beat

♩ = 2 beats

♩. = 3 beats

𝅗𝅥 = 4 beats

𝅗𝅥. = 6 beats

There are two accents to the measure:
a strong one on the first beat and
a weaker one on the fourth beat.

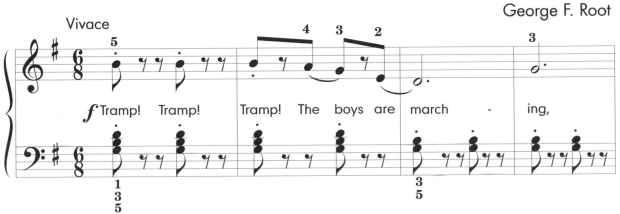

Tramp! Tramp! Tramp! The boys are march - ing,

Cheer up, com - rades, they will come. And be - neath the star-ry flag we shall

breathe the air a - gain of the free land in our own be - lov - ed home.

By Moonlight

Hand Position

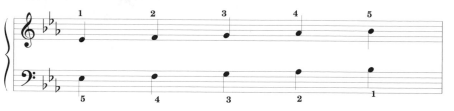

Andante   59/60

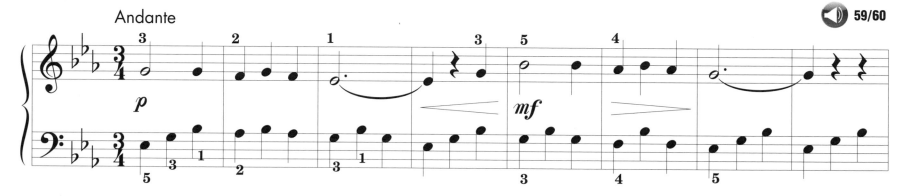

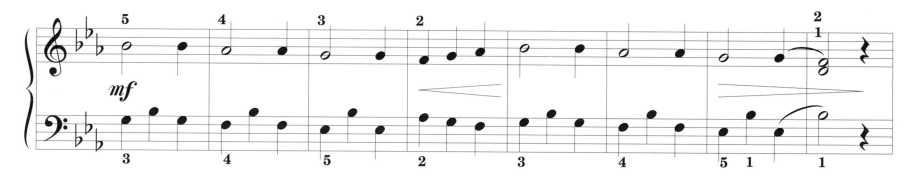

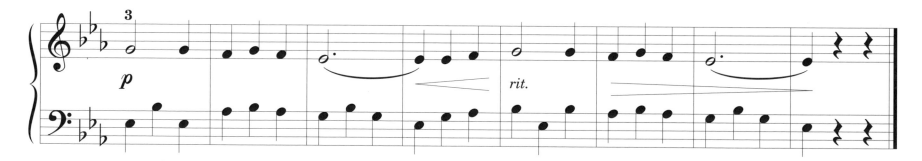

How D'ye Do?

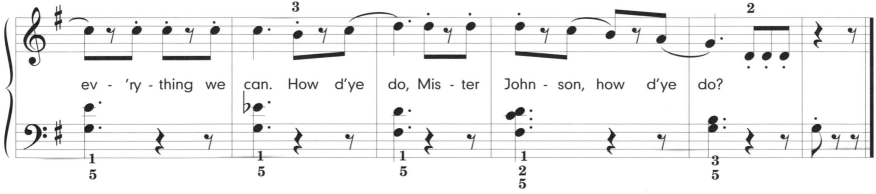

Scales and Chords
used in this book

C Major

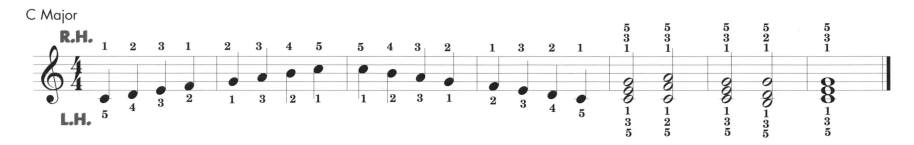

G Major

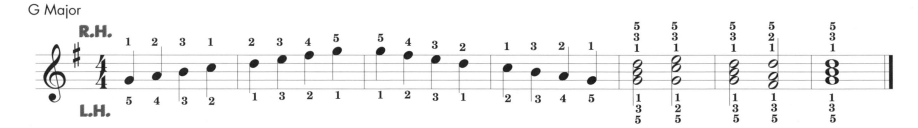

D Major

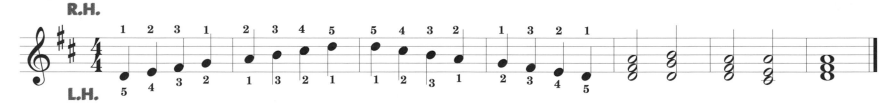

A Major

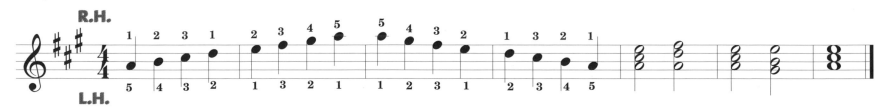

F Major

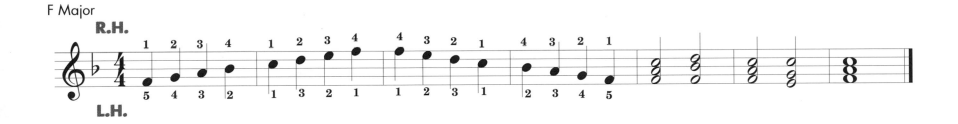

Bb Major

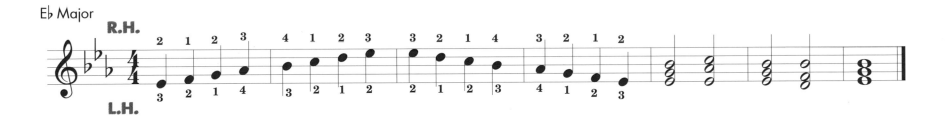

Eb Major

Glossary

of musical terms and expression marks used

> **(Accent)**	… special emphasis on a note or chord
Allegretto	… light and lively
Allegro	… fast
Andante	… slow
Andantino	… slow, but not as slow as andante
Animato	… animated
a tempo	… return to original speed
< **Crescendo**	… gradually louder
> **Decrescendo**	… gradually softer
Diminuendo	… softer by degrees
f – **Forte**	… loud
$f\!f$ – **Fortissimo**	… very loud
Legato	… smooth and connected
L.H.	… left hand
8va	… play one octave higher

mf – **Mezzo forte**	… moderately loud
mp – **Mezzo piano**	… moderately soft
Moderato	… moderately
⌢ **Pause**	… hold the note or chord longer according to taste
pp – **Pianissimo**	… very soft
p – **Piano**	… soft
Poco	… little
:‖	… repeat sign
R.H.	… right hand
Rit/Ritard	… gradually slower
⌒ **Slur**	… connected
Staccato	… detached, short
Tempo	… speed
Vivace	… fast and vivacious

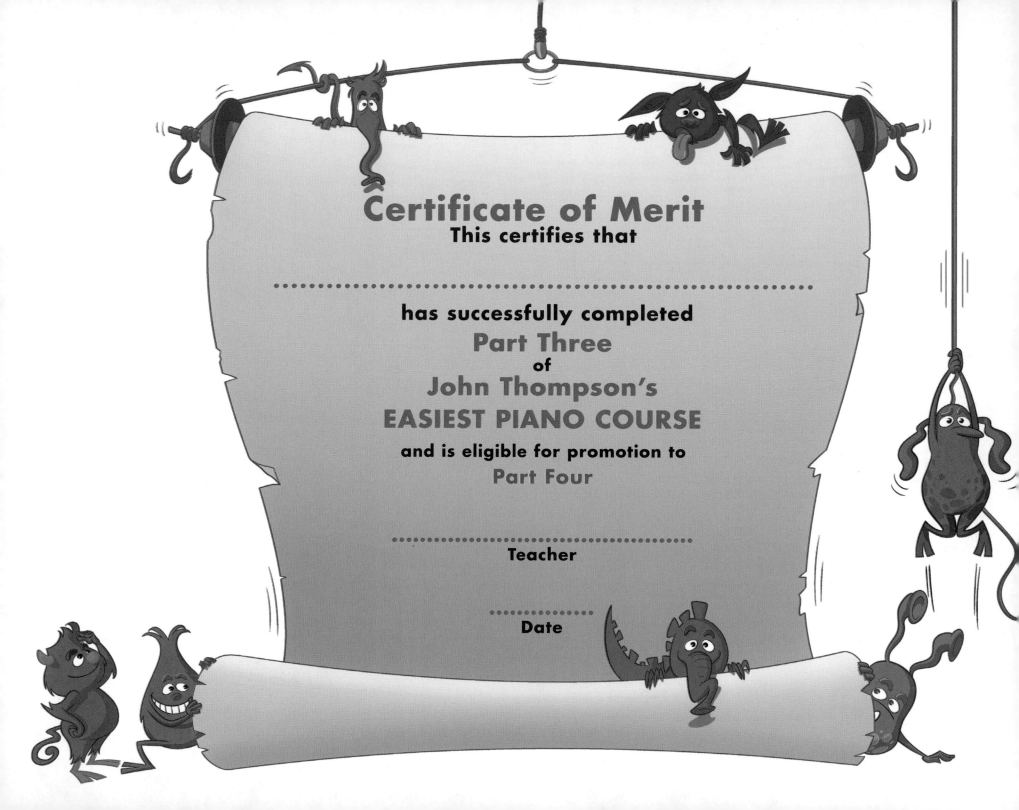

Certificate of Merit

This certifies that

....

has successfully completed
Part Three
of
John Thompson's
EASIEST PIANO COURSE

and is eligible for promotion to
Part Four

....

Teacher

....

Date